POP HITS
IN A
CLASSICAL
STYLE

Arranged by David Pearl

ISBN 978-1-70513-157-2

HAL•LEONARD®

Visit Hal Leonard Online at
www.halleonard.com

Contact us:
Hal Leonard
7777 West Bluemound Road
Milwaukee, WI 53213
Email: info@halleonard.com

In Europe, contact:
Hal Leonard Europe Limited
42 Wigmore Street
Marylebone, London, W1U 2RN
Email: info@halleonardeurope.com

In Australia, contact:
Hal Leonard Australia Pty. Ltd.
4 Lentara Court
Cheltenham, Victoria, 3192 Australia
Email: info@halleonard.com.au

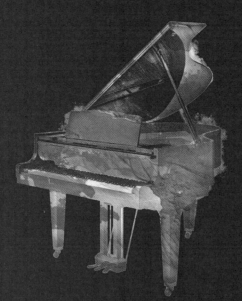

BIG GIRLS DON'T CRY

Words and Music by STACY FERGUSON
and TOBY GAD

Moderately

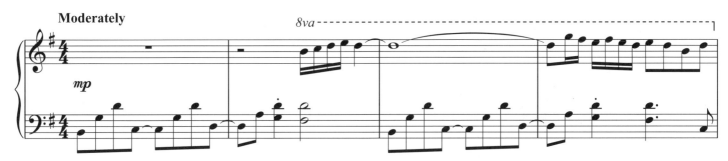

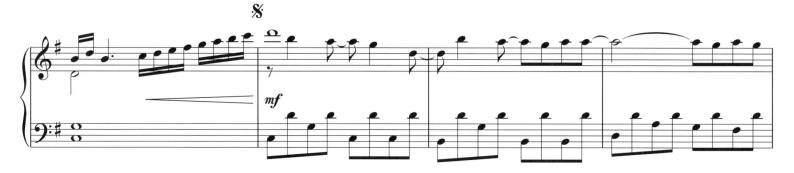

D.S. al Coda

CODA

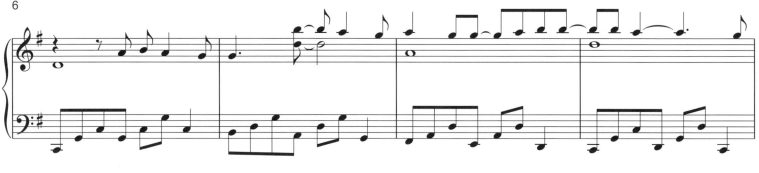

ALL OF ME

Words and Music by JOHN STEPHENS
and TOBY GAD

Moderately, freely moving

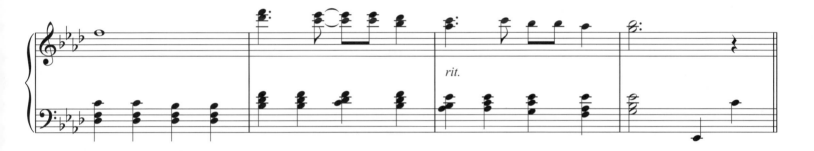

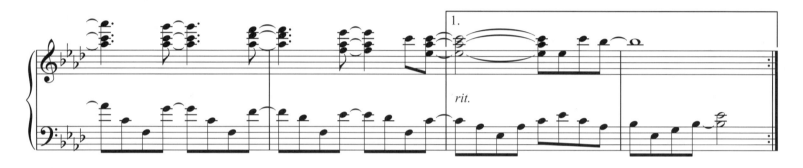

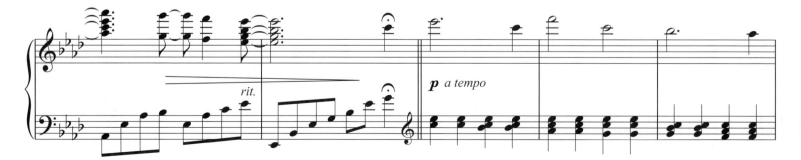

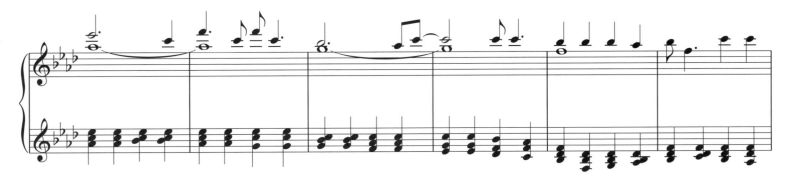

BEFORE HE CHEATS

Words and Music by JOSH KEAR
and CHRIS TOMPKINS

Moderately, in 2, with a flamenco-like passion

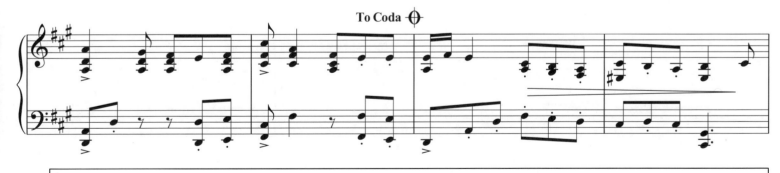

14

D.S. al Coda

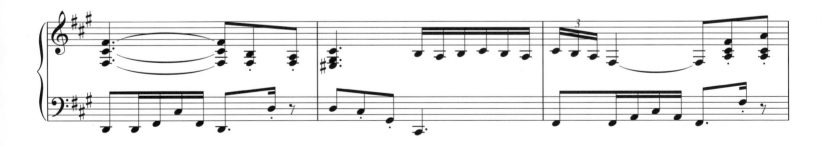

Much slower

BOULEVARD OF BROKEN DREAMS

Words by BILLIE JOE
Music by GREEN DAY

Moderately slow March tempo

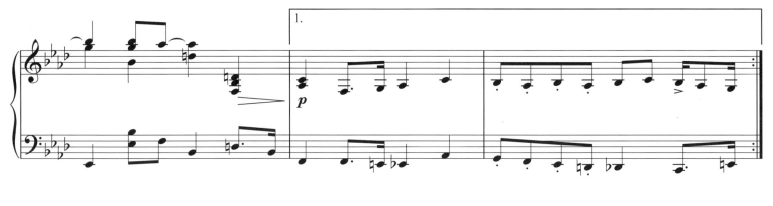

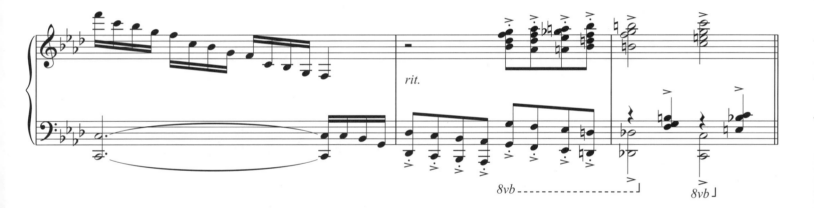

CALL ME MAYBE

Words and Music by CARLY RAE JEPSEN,
JOSHUA RAMSAY and TAVISH CROWE

Bright 4

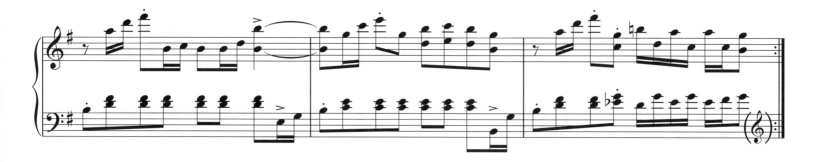

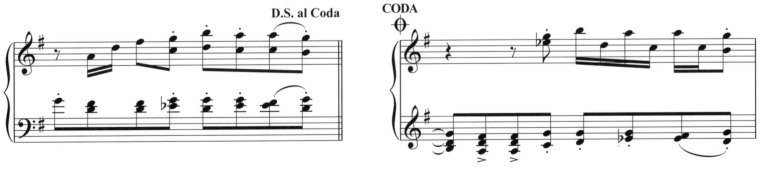

COUNT ON ME

Words and Music by BRUNO MARS,
ARI LEVINE and PHILIP LAWRENCE

Bright 4, "Classical Swing" style

(L.H. sim. throughout)

DESPACITO

Words and Music by LUIS FONSI,
ERIKA ENDER, JUSTIN BIEBER,
JASON BOYD, MARTY JAMES GARTON
and RAMÓN AYALA

Freely flowing

𝄋 Moderate Tango

rit. 　　　　mp *a tempo*

mf

To Coda $\oplus$

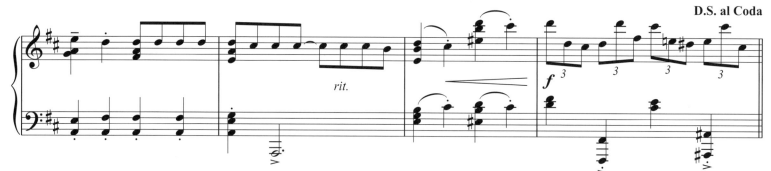

HAPPIER

Words and Music by MARSHMELLO,
STEVE MAC and DAN SMITH

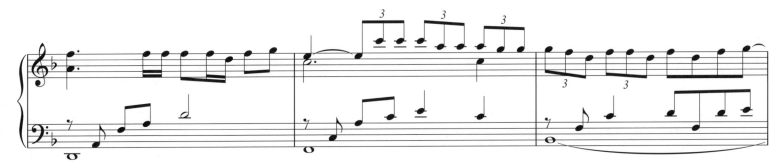

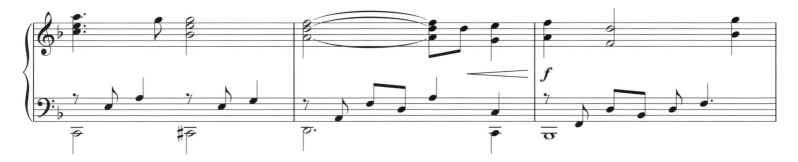

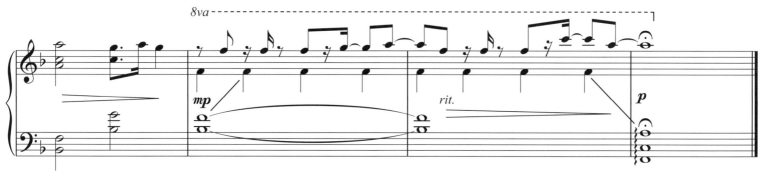

ROYALS

Words and Music by ELLA YELICH-O'CONNOR
and JOEL LITTLE

JAR OF HEARTS

Words and Music by BARRETT YERETSIAN,
CHRISTINA PERRI and DREW LAWRENCE

Slowly, steady

To Coda ⊕

D.S. al Coda

44

CODA

ROLLING IN THE DEEP

Words and Music by ADELE ADKINS
and PAUL EPWORTH

Moderately, with a driving beat

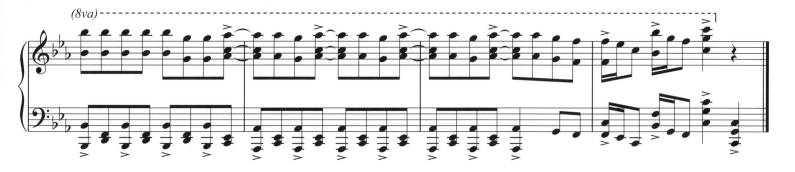

SHAKE IT OFF

Words and Music by TAYLOR SWIFT,
MAX MARTIN and SHELLBACK

To Coda ⊕ | 1. | 2.

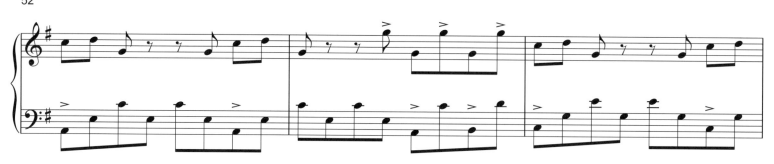

D.S. al Coda

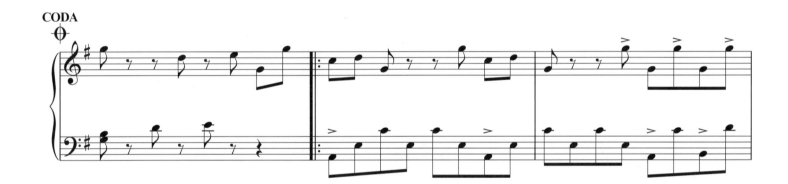

CODA

SOMEONE LIKE YOU

Words and Music by ADELE ADKINS
and DAN WILSON

Slowly, freely moving

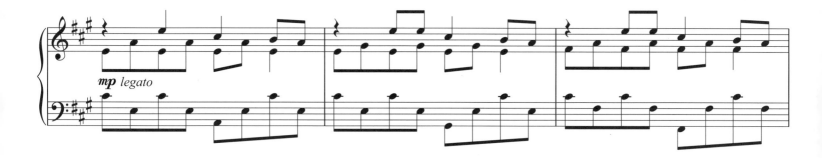

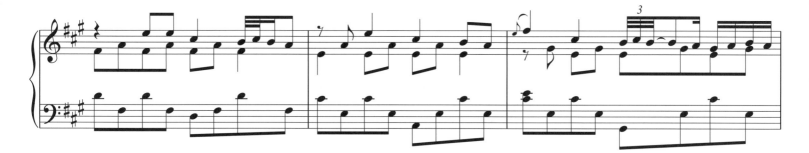

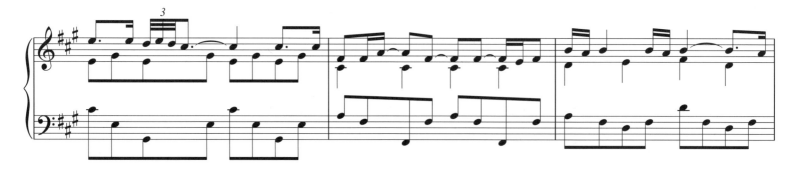

CODA

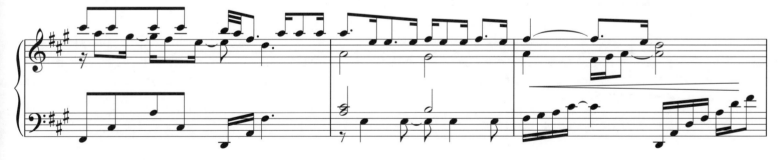

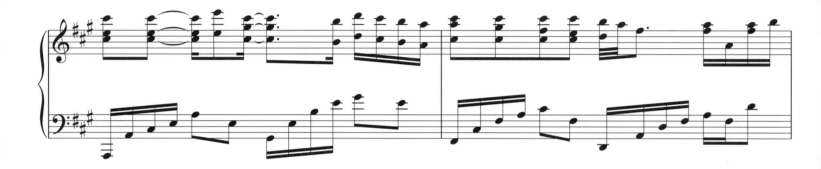

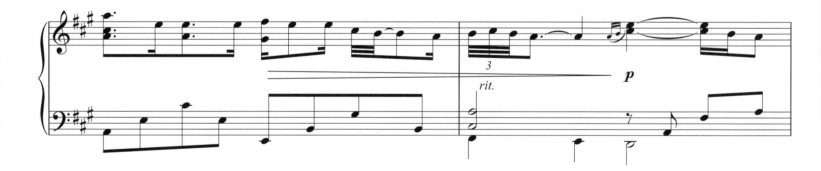

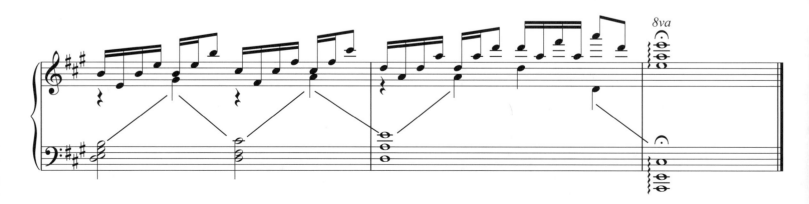

UPTOWN FUNK

Words and Music by MARK RONSON,
BRUNO MARS, PHILIP LAWRENCE,
JEFF BHASKER, DEVON GALLASPY,
NICHOLAUS WILLIAMS, LONNIE SIMMONS,
RONNIE WILSON, CHARLES WILSON,
RUDOLPH TAYLOR and ROBERT WILSON

Moderately fast

L.H. staccato

To Coda ⊕

D.S. al Coda

CODA

STACY'S MOM

Words and Music by CHRIS COLLINGWOOD
and ADAM SCHLESINGER

Moderately fast, pulsing

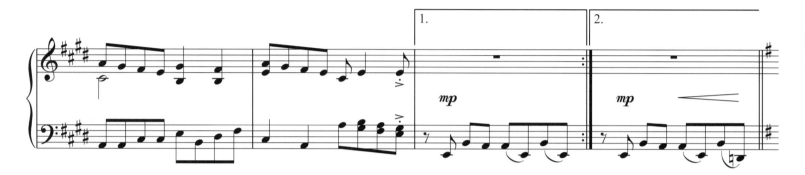

UNWRITTEN

Words and Music by NATASHA BEDINGFIELD,
DANIELLE BRISEBOIS and WAYNE RODRIGUES

Slowly, dreamily

Faster, building

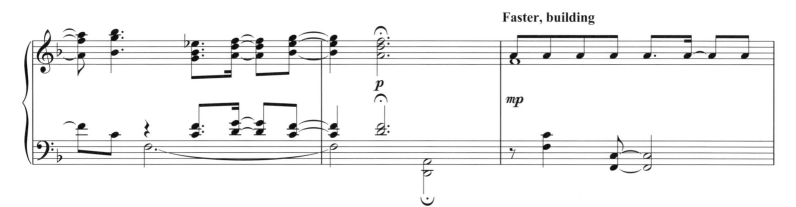

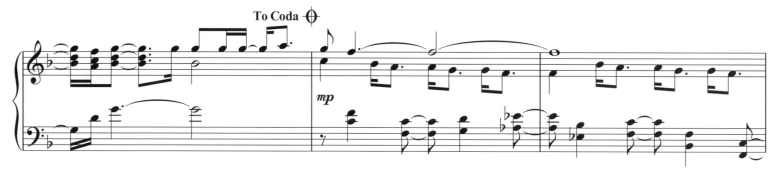

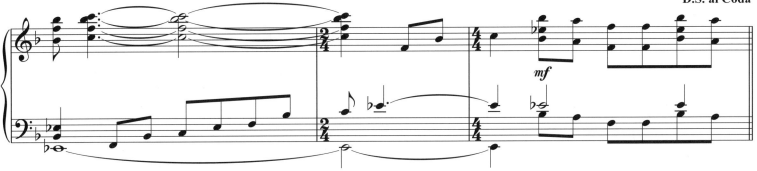

D.S. al Coda

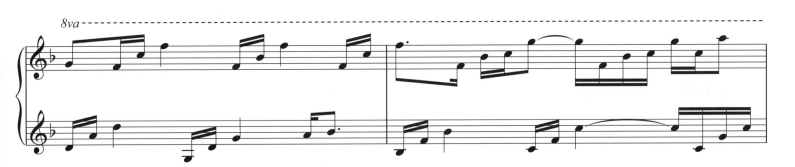

Looking to add some variety to your playing? Enjoy these beautifully distinctive arrangements for piano solo! These popular tunes get new and unique treatments for a fun and fresh presentation. Explore new styles and enjoy these favorites with a bit of a twist! Each collection includes 20 songs for the intermediate to advanced player.

BOHEMIAN RHAPSODY & OTHER EPIC SONGS

Band on the Run • A Day in the Life • Free Bird • November Rain • Piano Man • Roundabout • Stairway to Heaven • Take the Long Way Home • and more.

00196019 Piano Solo...**$14.99**

CHRISTMAS CAROLS

Away in a Manger • Deck the Hall • The First Noel • God Rest Ye Merry, Gentlemen • Hark! the Herald Angels Sing • It Came upon the Midnight Clear • Jingle Bells • Joy to the World • O Holy Night • Silent Night • Up on the Housetop • We Three Kings of Orient Are • What Child Is This? • and more.

00147214 Piano Solo...**$14.99**

CHRISTMAS COLLECTION

Blue Christmas • The Christmas Song (Chestnuts Roasting on an Open Fire) • Frosty the Snow Man • Here Comes Santa Claus (Right down Santa Claus Lane) • Let It Snow! Let It Snow! Let It Snow! • Silver Bells • Sleigh Ride • White Christmas • Winter Wonderland • and more.

00172042 Piano Solo...**$14.99**

CLASSIC ROCK

Another One Bites the Dust • Aqualung • Beast of Burden • Born to Be Wild • Carry on Wayward Son • Layla • Owner of a Lonely Heart • Roxanne • Smoke on the Water • Sweet Emotion • Takin' It to the Streets • 25 or 6 to 4 • Welcome to the Jungle • and more!

00138517 Piano Solo...**$14.99**

Prices, contents, and availability subject to change without notice.

DISNEY FAVORITES

Beauty and the Beast • Can You Feel the Love Tonight • Chim Chim Cher-ee • For the First Time in Forever • How Far I'll Go • Let It Go • Mickey Mouse March • Remember Me (Ernesto de la Cruz) • You'll Be in My Heart • You've Got a Friend in Me • and more.

00283318 Piano Solo...**$14.99**

JAZZ POP SONGS

Don't Know Why • I Just Called to Say I Love You • I Put a Spell on You • Just the Way You Are • Killing Me Softly with His Song • Mack the Knife • Michelle • Smooth Operator • Sunny • Take Five • What a Wonderful World • and more.

00195426 Piano Solo...**$14.99**

JAZZ STANDARDS

All the Things You Are • Beyond the Sea • Georgia on My Mind • In the Wee Small Hours of the Morning • The Lady Is a Tramp • Like Someone in Love • A Nightingale Sang in Berkeley Square • Someone to Watch Over Me • That's All • What'll I Do? • and more.

00283317 Piano Solo...**$14.99**

POP BALLADS

Against All Odds (Take a Look at Me Now) • Bridge over Troubled Water • Fields of Gold • Hello • I Want to Know What Love Is • Imagine • In Your Eyes • Let It Be • She's Got a Way • Total Eclipse of the Heart • You Are So Beautiful • Your Song • and more.

00195425 Piano Solo...**$14.99**

POP HITS

Billie Jean • Fields of Gold • Get Lucky • Happy • Ho Hey • I'm Yours • Just the Way You Are • Let It Go • Poker Face • Radioactive • Roar • Rolling in the Deep • Royals • Smells like Teen Spirit • Viva la Vida • Wonderwall • and more.

00138156 Piano Solo...**$14.99**

HAL•LEONARD®

www.halleonard.com